CREATING GROUPS

SAGE HUMAN SERVICES GUIDES, VOLUME 2

SAGE HUMAN SERVICES GUIDES

a series of books edited by ARMAND LAUFFER and published in cooperation with the University of Michigan School of Social Work.

CREATING GROUPS

by Harvey J. Bertcher
and
Frank F. Maple

VOLUME 2
SAGE HUMAN SERVICES GUIDES

Published in cooperation with the
University of Michigan School of Social Work

82-1924

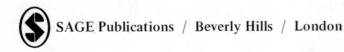

SAGE Publications / Beverly Hills / London

For information address:

SAGE Publications, Inc.
275 South Beverly Drive
Beverly Hills, California 90212

SAGE Publications Ltd
28 Banner Street
London EC1Y 8QE

Printed in the United States of America

Library of Congress Cataloging in Publication Data

Bertcher, Harvey J
   Creating groups.

  (Sage human services guides ; v. 2)
   1. Small groups—Programmed instruction. 2. Decision-making, Group—Programmed instruction. 3. Social group work—Programmed instruction. I. Maple, Frank F., joint author. II. Title.
HM133.B478   301.18'5'077   77-22401
ISBN 0-8039-0881-4

THIRD PRINTING, 1982

CONTENTS

CREATING GROUPS, like each of the *Sage Human Services Guides,* has been thoroughly tested and evaluated prior to publication.

The current text is a much expanded and modified version of a pamphlet used over a four year period with graduate students in social work and for inservice training with practitioners in a wide variety of social agency settings.

CREATING GROUPS is published by Sage Publications in collaboration with the Continuing Education Program in the Human Services of the University of Michigan School of Social Work. Armand Lauffer is Series Editor.

PREFACE

INTRODUCTION TO CREATING GROUPS

The effectiveness of any group is partially determined by the particular attributes or characteristics that each individual brings to the group. Ideally, this suggests that grouping people who have certain attributes should result in greater benefits for all group members than would any other mix. It is the purpose of this program to teach you how to understand and influence the composition of a group.

It is our impression that many people overlook or underestimate the powerful effect of a group's composition on the interaction that ensues. We also believe that people often ignore the potential benefits that could accrue from changing the make-up of the group once it has begun to meet. (The exception to this rule is the removal of the most obstreperous member.) Finally, we have been dissatisfied with our own vagueness when we presented material on this topic to our students.

In developing this program, we have drawn from studies in small group theory related to member characteristics that are viewed as influencing group effectiveness, as well as from research pertaining to group psychotherapy. We are far from satisfied with the material we located. The prediction of group effectiveness is a complex matter. Many of the studies that have been done in this area pertain to effectiveness in completing some discrete task, rather than focusing on the development of a group that is effective in bringing about change in the problematic social functioning of individual members. Nevertheless, we offer this program in the hope that it will enhance learning with regard to group composition.

It is our opinion that the program could also be useful to many persons involved in composing groups, e.g., a community organization worker putting together a task force, an administrator assembling a committee, an in-service trainer composing a class group, and others. Most of our examples refer to groups whose prime objective is to help each member cope more effectively with life situations that are currently or potentially problematic for them. But many groups exist to accomplish group goals, e.g., a committee that works to create a written report recommending policy changes. We believe that readers who are concerned with such groups will, by extension, find this program helpful to their endeavors.

This is a new and updated version of an earlier manuscript. Our students tell us that they found both content and format of the earlier version useful: in short, the program has stood the test of time surprisingly well. Nevertheless, we've made many adjustments in response to their recommendations.

Persons familiar with the earlier version will find a new and hopefully improved discussion of "Balance," a discussion of occasions when heterogeneity of descriptive attributes is appropriate, and a brief list of book chapters that review research on group composition. For the rest, changes have generally been designed to clarify particular wordings or concepts. We hope new readers will find it rewarding.

ACKNOWLEDGMENTS

We wish to express our appreciation to our faculty colleagues for many constructive suggestions. In particular, comments by Paul Glasser, Charles Wolfson and Maeda Galinsky have been most helpful. In addition, students too numerous to mention have provided valuable feedback. Henry Wallace joined this project following several revisions of the text and made invaluable changes in the format of the program. Four students in the School of Social Work, University of Michigan, participated in a final test of the program and made many useful suggestions; they were Rosemary Mackin, Linda Stanyar, Kathy Wong, and Daneen Woolson. We especially want to recognize the patience and fortitude of our secretaries, Pauline Bush, Sandra Smith and Joan Rosenwach for their support through several revisions of this document.

INSTRUCTIONAL OBJECTIVES

In reading this handbook you should be aware of our objectives and those which we have set out for you, the reader.

First, given a number of potential members for a particular kind of group that is to be created, and a description of pertinent attributes of each member, you should be able to define the purpose of the group in measurable terms, and then to select those attributes of the potential members which will be the best predictors of group effectiveness. Using these criteria, as well as other factors affecting group composition, e.g., group size, projected length of time the group will meet, etc., you should be able to compose a group in which the attributes of each member have either:

1) beneficial consequences for every other member of the group, or

2) an absence of serious negative consequences for every other member of the group.

Second, given an existing group (with all of the above information), you should be able to participate in the modification of existing group composition so that the attributes of each member have either:

1) beneficial consequences for every other member of the group, or

2) an absence of serious negative consequences for every other member of the group.

Now *that's* a mouthful. But since it's all in a good cause, and since you've read this far, you might as well give it a whirl. Good luck.

Ann Arbor, Michigan   H.J.B.
March 1977   F.F.M.

OBTAINING SPECIFIC INFORMATION

attributes: An attribute is any characteristic or quality by which an individual may be described and compared with others.

Of the two sets of attributes below,

1. Which is specific? _____
2. Which is non-specific and requires further definition?_____

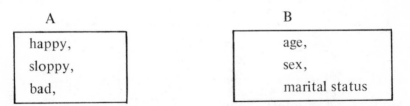

A	B
happy,	age,
sloppy,	sex,
bad,	marital status

descriptive attributes can be used to *classify* an individual.

behavioral attributes describe the way in which an individual acts, can act, or has acted.

Correct answers will always be given at the top of the next page. Please write your answers *before* turning the page. Otherwise you will weaken the effectiveness of this program.

Answers for page 11:

  1. B; 2. A   Good for you!

Please label the statements below:

    "B" for behavioral

    "D" for descriptive

| is 25 years old,

has completed 12 years of schooling.

has been a patient for two months. | refuses to play with the other nursery school children,

repeatedly asked to join the treatment group. |

1. _____ ?   2. _____ ?

| . . . ex-psychiatric hospital patient who doesn't have a job,

. . . runaway adolescent girl who is pregnant out of wedlock with no place to go. |

3. _____ ?

(Answers on page 13)

Please label these statements:

    "D" for descriptive attribute

    "B" for behavioral attribute

1. _____ usually takes a position and inflexibly defends it verbally in group discussions

2. _____ female

3. _____ 5' 11"

4. _____ impartially

5. _____ from Denver, Colorado

6. _____ seldom follows through on the task responsibilities given her in the group

7. _____ on probation as a ward of the court

8. _____ a member of the group

9. _____ could teach others to scuba dive

10. _____ is a scuba diver

Correct answers for page 12 are:

1. D; 2. B; 3. D

If some or *all* your answers disagree with ours, re-read the definitions on page 11.

In role theory terms, a descriptive attribute refers to a position an individual occupies. It can refer to a category of individuals who are similar in some respect, e.g., students, or to a condition or state of being, e.g., on probation.

A behavioral attribute refers to the way in which a person has performed, performs now, or could be expected to perform in a position, based on his past performance. It is stated in action terms.

Attributes must be stated clearly, that is, they must be either:

Descriptive: is a member of the Detroit Lions (a position)

or

Behavioral: plays aggressively (an aspect of role performance in a position)

Example: ". . . plays football for the Detroit Lions," is *not clear,* since it could refer to a position he occupies—player—or to his ability to play professional football.

Answers for pages 12 and 13:

1. B; 2. D; 3. D; 4. B; 5. D; 6. B; 7. D;
8. D; 9. B; 10. D.

Moral—Be specific! Use words that distinguish between position occupancy (a descriptive attribute) and the actual behavior in that position (a behavioral attribute).

PROBLEM: A student was asked to list five positions occupied by a friend of his and some aspects of the friend's role performance in these positions. Please indicate whether you agree "√" or disagree "X" with his choices.

Five positions held by my friend are:

1. _____ 24 year-old male

2. _____ red head

3. _____ 6′ 3″

4. _____ plays football aggressively

5. _____ scuba diver

Several aspects of his behavior in the positions he holds are:

6. _____ hits or wrestles in play with peers

7. _____ doesn't say much in group situations

8. _____ states feelings best in one-to-one situations

9. _____ says he would rather be alone than in groups

10. _____ is a problem drinker

Answers for page 14:

1. √; 2. √; 3. √; 4. √; 5. √; 6. √; 7. √; 8. √;
9. √; 10. X.

You may have had trouble with No. 10 but "is a problem drinker" refers to a condition, not an action.

Section 2

GROUP CREATION VS GROUP MODIFICATION

CREATION vs. MODIFICATION

You are most likely to use group composition skills and knowledge in carrying out two tasks: group creation and group modification.

In Group Creation, you select members for a group that doesn't yet exist. The potential members may have had little or no prior social contact as a group. As a result you literally "create" a group from a collection of people who are often strangers to one another. A group is created because:

1) you want participants to model for each other;
2) you want participants to reinforce each other;
3) you want a variety of ideas for problem solving, heightened awareness, learning, decision making, etc; or
4) you want an ongoing support system for members.

In Group Modification, the composition of an existing group is changed by adding new members (either because old members leave, or to increase the size of the group) or removing present members, in order to enable the members to achieve individual and/or group goals more effectively. Temporary modification involves:

15

1) holding one or more members out of a single meeting or a series of meetings

2) adding "visitors" to a meeting for some specific purpose

3) structuring meetings so that the group is purposely divided in some fashion.

Below are three examples of group composition.

Please label them:

"C" for group *creation*

"M" for group *modification*

---

1. A group worker spent several weeks getting to know and be accepted by members of a street corner gang. After they had agreed to work with him, he became aware of the fact that the group was too large, and suggested that the boys might want to cut the group's size.

---

1. This is an example of _____ (?)

---

2. A school social worker decided that some clients he was seeing individually could profit from being together in a treatment group. Accordingly, he invited seven fourth-grade boys who were on his caseload to form a group.

---

2. This is an example of _____ (?)

---

3. In a twenty-five bed tuberculosis ward a social worker proposed that five patients approaching discharge form a discharge-planning group to assist them with post-hospital problems.

---

3. This is an example of _____ (?)

(Answers on page 18)

GROUP CREATION

When creating a group, two kinds of attributes are particularly helpful:

1) selecting some members on the basis of previously demonstrated ability to perform either *task* or *group maintenance* roles in a group, i.e., behavioral attributes.

2) selecting members who can serve as good *models*[1] for others to emulate because they are similar to the other members, re descriptive attributes, or can do something well, re behavioral attributes.

Let's look at task and maintenance roles first. Research has indicated that a group needs at least two special functions to be performed if the group is to survive and develop. One function has to do with working toward the group's goal: this is the *task role.* The other involves keeping the group together as it works on achieving its goals by effecting compromises, soothing hurt feelings, making members feel important, etc: this is the *group maintenance role.*

When you include one or more individuals who have demonstrated good task role performance as well as some who have demonstrated effective maintenance role performance in the past, you help the group to survive and develop. There is one major exception to this: two very assertive specialists are likely to clash.

The kind of task role performance (or task leadership) needed is related both to the task itself and to the situation to which the task is addressed. For example, a person who has the behavioral attributes of being well-organized and purposeful *might* perform the task functions effectively for a time-limited group; but an individual who has many community contacts and knows how to use them *might* perform some of the essential task functions effectively for a group that is meeting in order to improve its members' use of community resources.

Group maintenance leadership functions on the other hand, are less a result of the task itself than of the behavioral attributes of

Answers for page 16:

1. M 2. C 3. C —You might quibble with this last answer (3), but remember that the discharge group would come into existence for a new and different purpose than that which characterizes the ward, and would not include all of the patients on the ward.

members. For example, in a group with a few verbally aggressive members, a few calm, quiet members may be able to help the group navigate troubled waters, but on the other hand, if group members are reluctant to participate, members who can crack jokes in a tense situation could ease the situation, with a resultant increase in participation.

NOTE

1. For example, see Harvey Bertcher, Jesse Gordon, Michael E. Hayes, and Harry Mial, *Role Modeling Role Playing: A Manual for Vocational Development and Employment Agencies.* Ann Arbor: Manpower Science Services, Inc. 1970, pp. 85-99.

Section 3

MODELING

MODELING

Modeling refers to a process in which an individual learns new behaviors by imitating the behaviors of another person and then adapting the observed demonstration to his or her own style.

> Example: Albert might be selected for group membership because he has the behavioral attribute of being able to control his temper. This may be important because another member, Bill, does not control his temper, and needs to see how it's done effectively by a peer.

> Example: Ms. Herman might be selected for a group of psychiatric hospital patients who are approaching discharge because she has had considerable work experience, has been out of the hospital for six months and is doing quite well, is interested in participating, and the group will be attempting to increase the employability of its members.

This latter example suggests an often overlooked point: in looking for members, don't limit yourself to clients of your agency or to people in your immediate population. People who have "graduated" are an excellent potential source of models who can help the group; in addition *they* can benefit from being in the position of helping others.

Moral: don't limit your group creation horizons. Think big!

19

REVIEW

In short, individuals may be chosen for group membership because of: task/maintenance, involving their demonstrated ability to provide task or maintenance functions and/or model, involving a specific skill or personality trait that makes them an appropriate model for others.

Problem: You are working in a large correctional institution for adolescent girls. The staff has decided that a discharge planning group of twelve (the entire population of the pre-release cottage) would be too large for individualization. As a result, two groups of six are being planned to prepare the girls for return to the community. The following is some brief (and admittedly limited) information about some descriptive and behavioral attributes of the twelve girls. Please read them and then, based on the information given, answer the questions below. (Note that more than one answer is possible for questions 2, 3, and 4.)

MARY: quiet, shy, but well liked by the girls.

JANE: Comes up with great ideas but doesn't follow through on them.

BERTHA: a few years older, and engages in helpful "mothering" of the younger girls. During her stay, she has greatly improved her relations with her parents.

ANNETTE: snappish, experiencing considerable physical discomfort due to her asthma.

GINNY: very bitter about her situation, blaming everyone for her problems. She has a "chip on her shoulder" attitude toward girls and staff alike.

NAOMI: extremely efficient in organizing cigarette smuggling into the institution.

LINDA: nervous and high strung—her runaway and subsequent pregnancy have created great friction with her family.

SUZY: well liked, attractive, known for her many kindnesses to the other girls.

BARBARA: depressed and worried about her future. She stays away from other girls.

POLLY: a college student, formerly president of a sorority and now organizer of cottage parties.

JOANN: looking forward to finishing high school at the institution. She is the "sunshine kid" whose cheerful optimism makes her attractive to the other girls.

BETTY: has fought with as many people as she could since the day she arrived, usually with words, occasionally with hair pulling and fists.

Two girls who have demonstrated task role ability are

1. _____ , _____

Three girls who have demonstrated group maintenance role ability are

2. _____, _____ , _____

3. Joann could be a good model for (which girls) _____ , _____ with regard to optimistic outlook.

4. Suzy could be a good model for Betty with regard to_____ _____ (behavior).

5. _____could be a good model for_____ with regard to communication-with-family behavior.

Answers follow.

Answers for Problem:
1. Naomi and Polly; 2. Bertha, Suzy and Joann and perhaps Mary; 3. Barbara, Annette, or Ginny; 4. kindness or some similar word; 5. Bertha, Linda

Note: In answering 1, you may have decided that Naomi could be a good task leader but a poor model. Sharpies like *you* are always going to rush ahead. Be patient and we'll get to that issue.

REVIEW

1. Group effectiveness is partially determined by the attributes that each individual brings to the group.
2. The attributes of an individual can be described in two ways: descriptive attributes that can be used to classify an individual's *position, state* or *condition*, or behavioral attributes that describe the ways in which an individual *acts, can act,* or *has acted.*

We used to think that descriptive attributes were the most useful in selecting group members: research indicates that behavioral attributes are much better predictors of an individuals behavior in a group.

EFFECTIVE GROUPS

EFFECTIVE GROUPS

Effective groups tend to be groups in which members are:

Interactive: members talk to each other; many ideas or viewpoints are exchanged.

Compatible: members show that they like one another through reinforcing behaviors.

Responsive: members are interested and active in helping one another; models of helping and being helped are available in the group.

Research indicates[2] that you are more likely to have an effective group if the members are: (a) homogeneous with regard to descriptive attributes and (b) heterogeneous with regard to behavioral attributes. Common descriptive attributes help to foster interactiveness and the development of compatibility. For example, a young adult in conflict with his parents would probably not be a very compatible, interactive, or responsive member of a social club for senior citizens.

Please complete the following analysis table for the group meetings by using:

"√" for groups showing the particular aspect of effectiveness.

"X" for groups lacking the particular aspect of effectiveness.

"?" for situations where there isn't enough information.

	Group A	Group B	Group C
INTERACTIVENESS			
COMPATIBILITY			
RESPONSIVENESS			

Here are descriptions of 3 groups:

Group A   As they talked, members discovered that each had, at one time, spent time in a psychiatric hospital. However, they were not yet interested in helping one another.

Group B   During the meeting, all of the boys continually yelled and screamed at one another. No decisions were made and several fist fights erupted. Finally, the leader sent the members home.

Group C   In the group meeting, each member concentrated on finishing his own project; there was no talking among the boys.

(Answers on page 26)

Heterogeneous behavioral attributes, on the other hand, make it possible for members to be responsive to one another constructively.

Example: For a group of ex-psychiatric hospital patients in a day-care program, it could be useful to have a member with the behavioral attribute of having recently taken up an engrossing new hobby that he actively shares with the group; another member who can use his behavioral attribute of executive ability to help organize the group; still another member who has the behavioral attribute of being able to put people at their ease, and so forth.

If everyone in the group has similar behavioral attributes (as well as similar descriptive attributes), has tried the same solutions and experienced the same failures, it may look like an unattractive group to people who are seeking answers for themselves.

SUMMARY

When creating a group, the potential members should have similar descriptive attributes but different behavioral attributes. Similar descriptive attributes will set the stage for interaction and the development of compatibility; different behavioral attributes make it likely that each individual will have something useful to contribute to others so that the interaction is "responsive."

Below is a list of attributes that characterize a number of prospective group members. On which should members be similar (homogeneous) and on which should they be different (heterogeneous)?

	HOMOGENEOUS (similar)	HETEROGENEOUS (different)	
1.			Age
2.			Talkativeness
3.			Highest school grade attained
4.			Fighting ability
5.			Tells jokes
6.			Seeks the opinions of others
7.			Marijuana user
8.			Probationary status

If you're thinking that this leaves out other considerations, you're right. Good thinking! Play along with us for now—there's lots more to come. (Answers on page 29.)

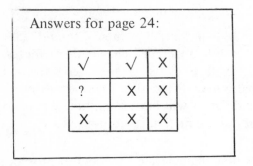

Answers for page 24:

√	√	X
?	X	X
X	X	X

BARRIERS TO EFFECTIVE GROUPS

Some compositional factors that *hinder* the development of effective groups are:

(A) Too much compatibility.
Example: Members of a street gang went to camp and were allowed to stay together in one cabin. They were able to resist effectively all efforts to use the camp experience to modify their behavior, and succeeded in terrorizing and dominating the other campers.

(B) Too (much/little) stress.
Example: Several members of a social club for adult ex-psychiatric hospital patients were unable to handle the slightest hint of criticism.

(C) Not enough role models of desired behavior.
Example: In a cottage of a boys' correctional institution, the members varied along a continuum of good to poor fighting ability. The cottage, however, had no one who could negotiate disputes, use humor to ease tense situations, keep his temper in an argument, etc.

(D) Negative sub-groups
Example: In one group of school malperformers, four of the members had come from the same neighborhood. Within the group they supported one another in sabotaging group purpose, victimizing individual members, controlling shared decision-making processes, etc.

In the examples that follow, refer to the previous descriptions to indicate the barrier(s) to group effectiveness listed (A, B, C, and/or D) for each group.

(Note that more than one answer is possible. Since the examples are brief, the amount of information is necessarily concise. Base your answers on the data as given.)

---

1. In terms of behavioral attributes, all of the potential members had demonstrated destructive acting-out behavior in social situations.

---

1. The barrier(s) to effectiveness in this group is (are) _____ .

---

2. At a child guidance clinic, five boys between the ages of ten and twelve reinforced one another's hostile behavior. They acted lika a gang when together.

   The clinic sent them to summer camp as a "morale-building-experience." At camp, these boys were placed in a cabin with five other boys who were all strangers to one another.

---

2. The barrier(s) to effectiveness in this group is (are) _____ .

---

3. The group was ten men: the total population of a group foster home, sponsored by a psychiatric hospital.

   The men tacitly agreed that it would be inadvisable to discuss their grievances against the woman in charge of the home, in spite of her punitive behavior, because they were afraid she would retaliate.

---

3. The barrier(s) to effectiveness in this group is (are) _____ :

> 4. All of the members of a married couples' group were very passive in conversation.

4. The barrier(s) to effectiveness in this group is (are) _____ .

(Answers on page 30)

NICE TO KNOW

During a research study,[3] male psychiatric hospital patients in a Veterans Hospital were observed and scored for "social activity," i.e., the degree to which they talked to others, were chosen by others, spoke in group meetings, and were helpful task group members (all **behavioral attributes**). Four kinds of groups were then created as follows:

SOCIAL ACTIVITY

	high	low
HOMOGENEOUS ATTRIBUTES	1. all above the average	2. all below the average
HETEROGENEOUS ATTRIBUTES	3. 2/3 above the average, 1/3 below	4. 1/3 above the average, 2/3 below

After making sure that there were no significant differences between members of any one of the four groups as to the **descriptive attributes** of age, length of stay in the hospital and living situation prior to hospitalization, the researchers found the "heterogeneous-high" group (#3) to be significantly better than all others at complex problem-solving and general performance.

In other words, starting with a group that by definition was fairly homogeneous with regard to descriptive attributes, and using knowledge of the social activity **(behavioral attributes)** of each member, it was possible to *predict* which group would be most effective at problem solving.

Answers for pages 27 and 28:

	Homogeneous	Heterogeneous
1.	√	
2.		√
3.	√	
4.		√
5.		√
6.		√
7.	√	
8.	√	

Answers for page 28:

1. C, A; 2. D; 3. B (too little stress), C; 4. C.

NOTES

2. For example, see Arnold P. Goldstein, Kenneth Heller and Lee B. Sechrest, *Psychotherapy and the Psychology of Behavioral Change.* New York: John Wiley and Sons, 1969, p. 325.

3. George W. Fairweather, *Social Psychology in Treating Mental Illness; An Experimental Approach.* New York: John Wiley, 1964, pp. 196-209.

Section 5

BALANCE

BALANCE

As mentioned before, the most effective groups are those whose members are different (heterogeneous) with respect to behavioral attributes. Heterogeneity implies not only difference, but balance: that is, a mix in which members fall along a "linear continuum" on critical behavioral attributes.[4] The continuum we have in mind is of the "never-sometimes-always" variety, or, stated more fully, each member could be rated on the following continuum in relation to his or her performance of particular behaviors:

Almost Never	Infrequently	Sometimes	Frequently	Almost Always
1	2	3	4	5

Imagine a group to be formed in an institution for adolescent unwed mothers: the problematic behavior that had led to the creation of a group was the consistent violation of doctor's orders by several girls. "Conforming to doctor's orders" constituted a critical attribute. Conforming to doctor's orders includes eating only

31

the right foods, engaging in appropriate exercise, getting sufficient rest, etc. As adolescents, however, several girls had trouble with authority figures, such as doctors; in addition, they failed to understand the potentially dangerous consequences to them and their babies of ignoring doctor's orders.

Accordingly, the Group Worker's task was to first rate each member in relation to the critical behavioral attribute (conforms to doctor's orders), and then determine which potential members would form the most balanced group in relation to *this attribute only* (for the moment).

Here is a list of nine pregnant girls and the Group Worker's assessment of their conformity to doctor's orders. Six of them have been rated and located on the linear continuum at the bottom of the page. Please do this for the other three. These descriptions are admittedly brief: it's often necessary to seek for more data to make such a rating. In this case, however, it's OK to rate speculatively, using the data we've provided.

__1__	Jane: Repeatedly eats junk foods although she has been told not to do so.
__4__	Bea: Wasn't getting enough exercise last month, but became more active after seeing her doctor.
__2__	Sue: Likes to sneak late reading, even though it's "lights out" at 10 p.m.
__3__	Maude: Often goes along with medical advice, but just as often uses her own judgment.
__?__	Mabel: Does just what the doctor tells her to do.
__1__	Cookie: Is defiant of doctor's orders to the point of doing the exact opposite of whatever she's told to do.
__?__	Ann: Follows doctor's orders some of the time but can be easily led astray by other girls.
__5__	Louise: Other girls see her as "goody goody" who never thinks for herself, just does what doctor tells her to do.
__?__	Sarah: Follows doctor's orders only when she's afraid that staff will catch her disobeying.

Conforms to Doctor's Orders

Almost Never	Infrequently	Sometime	Frequently	Almost Always
1	2	3	4	5
Jane Cookie	Sue	Maude	Bea	Louise

___1___ Jane

___4___ Bea

___2___ Sue

___3___ Maude

___5___ Mabel

___1___ Cookie

___2___ Ann

___5___ Louise

___2___ Sarah

Conforms to Doctor's Orders

Almost Never	Infrequently	Sometime	Frequently	Almost Always
1	2	3	4	5
Jane Cookie	Sue Ann Sarah	Maude	Bea	Louise Mabel

Although nine girls are eligible, the Group Worker has decided
that a group of six would be more workable, in order to make it
easier for each member to participate actively. Using the continuum from the previous page, which of these groups would represent the best balance of the behavioral attribute "conforms to
doctor's orders," A, B, or C?

Possible Grouping A

Almost Never	Infrequently	Sometime	Frequently	Almost Always
1	2	3	4	5
Jane Cookie	Sue		Bea	Louise Mabel

Possible Grouping B

Almost Never	Infrequently	Sometime	Frequently	Almost Always
1	2	3	4	5
Jane	Sue Sarah	Maude	Bea	Mabel

Possible Grouping C

Almost Never	Infrequently	Sometime	Frequently	Almost Always
1	2	3	4	5
Jane Cookie	Sarah	Maude	Bea	Louise

<u>   B   </u> would be the most balanced group with regard to the critical attribute "conforms to doctor's orders." Jane *and* Cookie would unbalance this group in the direction of too much defiance of doctor's order, particularly in group C, where Sarah could be easily influenced by Jane and Cookie.

Given the focus on one critical attribute, it is also necessary to attend to other behavioral attributes when creating a group. For example, the ability to ask the doctor questions when he was advising a girl had been observed to be associated with her conformity to his orders: the more questions asked, and well answered, the more likely the girl would be to conform to orders. Suppose that the Group Worker rated each girl with regard to the attribute "is able to ask appropriate questions when seeing the doctor," and came out with the following continuum:

Ability to Question Doctor

Almost Never	Infrequently	Sometime	Frequently	Almost Always
1	2	3	4	5
Jane	Ann	Sue	Sarah	Bea
Cookie	Louise	Maude		Mabel

The Group Worker compared his ratings by putting them side by side and averaging them.

	Conforms to doctor's orders	Ability to question doctor	Average rating
Jane	1	2	1.5
Bea	4	5	4.5
Sue	2	3	2.5

Maude	3	3	3
Mabel	5	5	5
Cookie	1	1	1
Ann	2	2	2
Louise	5	2	3.5
Sarah	2	4	3

```
  |           |           |           |           |
1 |     2     |     3     |     4     |     5     |
  |           |           |           |           |
```

Cookie Jane   Ann   Sue   Maude   Louise   Bea Mabel
                                Sarah

In trying to determine the best balance of critical behavioral attributes, the Group Worker found that Maude had demonstrated effective "task" skills in a party planning committee, and that Sarah had been observed mediating effectively when the girls hassled each other. Using all of this data, who would you select for a balanced group?

(Answers on page 38)

Note: Remember our earlier point about the use of former members as "helpers" and "models." Lest we give the impression that we've forgotten this, let us remind you that the eventual composition of this group might well profit from the inclusion of such a girl.

Let's now focus on a topic we've mentioned briefly: critical attributes.

NOTE

4. We are indebted to our colleagues, Paul Glasser and Sallie Churchill for the basic idea behind the approach we are about to describe.

Answer for page 36:

Jane, Ann, Maude, Sarah, Bea and Mabel. Cookie was
eliminated as too extreme; Maude and Sarah were chosen
over Sue and Louise because of their "task" and "socio-
emotional" skills respectively.

SELECTING CRITICAL ATTRIBUTES

CRITICAL ATTRIBUTES

Every human being can be characterized in terms of an enormous number of attributes. It is virtually impossible to create groups whose members are similar on *all* descriptive attributes and different on *all* behavioral attributes. Fortunately only a few attributes are *critical* for the development of an effective group.

SELECTING CRITICAL ATTRIBUTES

In creating the group of unwed mothers, the girls could have been classified according to such descriptive attributes as race, socio-economic status, educational attainment, number and age of siblings, place of birth, etc., and such behavioral attributes as enjoying long walks, knitting skillfully, being very possessive of friends, participating actively in group singing, etc. The basic question is: how do you know which of these are critical attributes for *this* group?

The major criterion for the selection of critical attributes is *group objective.* Group Objective means those things each member should be able to do acceptably well as a result of being in the group. In social work practice, a group's objective may be based on an agency's view of the needs of several clients or potential clients. In non-social work groups, the group's objective may be to represent constituencies in a larger group. Once the group begins, the members themselves may negotiate a modification of this objective with the leader. Group objective, to be useful, must be stated in measurable terms, otherwise no one can be sure it has been achieved.

EXAMPLES OF GROUP OBJECTIVE[5]

1) Members of a group of unemployed men should be able to find and hold a job.

2) Members of a street corner gang should avoid antisocial acts, and should instead perform prosocial acts.

3) Members of a group of classroom malperformers should want to improve all of their grades to a passing level.

A social worker in a home for unwed mothers (population 120, age range of residents thirteen to thirty with an average age of fifteen, typically entering the home in their sixth month of pregnancy) decided to create a discussion group whose objective was to cut down or eliminate violations of doctor's orders with regard to good pre-natal care, e.g., eating inappropriate foods, getting insufficient rest, etc. This group was created because several girls were not following the doctor's orders, presenting a definite health hazard for themselves and their babies. Using this limited information, what are some attributes that you would select as being "critical" to the achievement of the group's purpose?

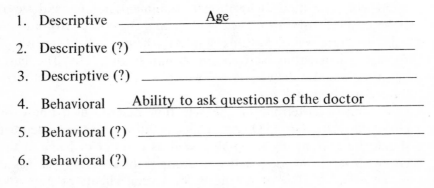

1. Descriptive _____Age_____

2. Descriptive (?) _____

3. Descriptive (?) _____

4. Behavioral ___Ability to ask questions of the doctor_____

5. Behavioral (?) _____

6. Behavioral (?) _____

(Answer on page 42)

NOTE

5. A more thorough examination of this important point can be found in Robert F. Mager, *Developing Instructional Objectives,* Palo Alto: Fearon Publishers, 1962. A briefer 5-page discussion of objectives is in Robert F. Mager, *Developing Attitude Toward Learning,* Palo Alto: Fearon Publishers, 1968, pp. 13-17.

Answers for page 40:

2. length of time before delivery; 3. physical condition; 5. eating habits; 6. behavior with regard to doctor's orders.

You may have thought of some additional responses, but if you included most of these, yours are probably appropriate.

Section 7

GROUP DEVELOPMENT

A second consideration in designating particular attributes as "critical" is group development, i.e., attributes that will facilitate the development of an effective group. As we indicated earlier, this includes behavioral attributes such as the ability to perform task or group maintenance acts, and model desired behaviors. Sometime individuals are included because they can help the group to grow. In this case, membership of particular individuals, while initially counterindicated, becomes appropriate in the interest of group development.

> Example: Several boys who had been involved in assorted illegal activities were placed on probation, and worked with as a group. One boy who was a ward of the court because of parental neglect was placed in the group because of his group maintenance attributes, e.g., good sense of humor, ability to get along well with everyone, etc. The group's purpose did not fit him; he had no history of antisocial behavior, but it provided him with a chance to be helpful and make some new friends.

> Example: The Community Center organized a social club for teenagers to help them develop skills in building relationships with members of the opposite sex. A girl who had served as president of a similar group a year earlier was invited to join the group both to assume some task leadership and show, by example, how members could manage their own group.

GATHERING SPECIFIC INFORMATION

Once critical attributes have been selected in relation to group objective and group development, the Group Worker should learn as much as he or she can about the degree to which each potential member shows these attributes in settings similar to the actual setting in which the group will be meeting.

One approach to obtaining this information is to develop a list of specific questions about actual attributes which can be asked of persons who have seen the potential member function in group situations. In this way, they can share with you their view of him or her with regard to critical attributes of the projected group. Another approach involves assigning a member to a short term group, e.g., group orientation to the agency, in which information about behavioral attributes is a useful by-product. A third approach would be for you to have an individual interview with the potential member.

Inaccurate or incomplete information has been known to lead to unhappy results. For example, someone tells you that a particular boy is very good at effecting compromises. He sounds like someone who could play a group maintenance role, and serve as a model for less patient boys. In your first group meeting you discover that he does this by beating up everyone who disagrees with him. Unfortunately, behavioral information, i.e., information about someone's ways of interacting with peers, is often not obtained when social workers compile a diagnostic statement. By now, however, it should be clear to you that it's crucial to have accurate factual data on behavioral attributes.

REVIEW: (Refer back to pages 39-44 if necessary)

1. The first major criterion for the selection of critical attributes is _____ .

2. The second major criterion is _____ .

3. In order to gather the necessary behavioral information about a potential member, it may be necessary to have him _____ a group meeting.

4. A potential group member who shows much more (or much less) of a critical attribute than any of the other potential members (should/should not_____ be included in the group.

(Answer on page 46)

USING GROUP OBJECTIVE

The *first* step in selecting members for a group is to specify the objective of the group. Groups have been created for the purpose of: helping the residents of a correctional institution develop specific plans for their return to the community; helping a group of senior citizens develop projects that will keep them in touch with community life; providing an opportunity for girls who are pregnant out-of-wedlock to receive information about and explore the alternatives available to them regarding adoption, or keeping their babies, so that each of them can make an informed decision concerning their baby's future, etc.

In each case, someone, the agency, the Group Worker, significant others, and/or the members, becomes aware of a problem shared by a number of members (or potential members) that might be helped through a group experience. In each case, the objective of the group refers *specifically* to changes in problematic attributes of the potential group members in the natural environment, i.e., outside of the group.

A juvenile court worker has decided to develop a treatment groups for boys who had been made wards of the court. From a list of fifty who are wards of the court, he has decided to choose eight. Some of the fifty boys are court wards because they have broken laws (auto theft, gang fights, etc.); others are wards because of unhealthy family conditions (neglect, abuse, etc.) although they themselves have broken no laws. The group objective is to minimize or eliminate delinquent behavior and replace it with pro-social behavior, so that probation can be terminated. In terms of descriptive attributes alone, which selection would be best?

Answers for page 45:

1. group objective; 2. group development; 3. observe
4. should not

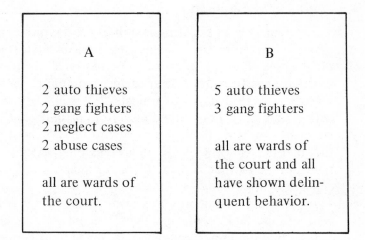

A	B
2 auto thieves	5 auto thieves
2 gang fighters	3 gang fighters
2 neglect cases	
2 abuse cases	all are wards of
	the court and all
all are wards of	have shown delin-
the court.	quent behavior.

(Answers on page 50)

Turn back to the description of the group for unwed mothers on page 40 then answer the following questions.

Of the descriptive attributes listed below, which one (or ones) would you select as critical on the basis of *group objective*? (cut down or eliminate violations of doctor's orders).

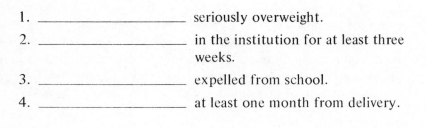

1. _____ seriously overweight.

2. _____ in the institution for at least three weeks.

3. _____ expelled from school.

4. _____ at least one month from delivery.

Of the behavioral attributes listed below, which would you select as critical on the basis of *group objective*?

5. _____ ignored or defied the doctor by not observing dietary restrictions.

6. _____ had heard there might be a group and asked to be included.

7. _____ had demonstrated good social skills in other groups.

8. _____ encouraged other girls to disregard doctor's orders.

(See page 48 for correct answers)

Now, imagine that you are working in a mental hospital, planning for a group whose objective is to assist patients in preparing for discharge. What are three descriptive attributes and three behavioral attributes of patients or ex-patients that would be useful in selecting members for such a group? (We'll give you one answer as a model for yours.)

Descriptive Attributes

1. Patients who are seen by staff as being within two or three months of being discharged.

2.

3.

Behavioral Attributes

4.

5.

6.

Answers for pages 46 and 47

CRITICAL DESCRIPTIVE ATTRIBUTES

1. __Yes__ ————————————————→ Good. This is a significant symptom of a girl who is not properly controlling calorie intake as ordered by the doctor.

2. __Yes__ ————————→ They have been present long enough for rule violation to be observed as a consistent pattern. Good.

3. __No__ ———————————————→ No clear relation to the problem behavior. Sorry.

4. __Yes__ ——————→ Right. They will not be leaving the group too quickly.

CRITICAL BEHAVIORAL ATTRIBUTES

5. __Yes__ ————————→ This is exactly the behavior to be modified. Fine.

6. __No__ ————————————————→ No clear relation to the group objective. Sorry.

7. __No__ ———————————→ Maybe later when *group development* is considered but not just now, since it's GROUP OBJECTIVE we're considering at the moment. Nice try, though.

8. __Yes__ ————————————————→ These girls are helping to create and/or maintain the problem the group is designed to eradicate. Good choice.

This is a difficult question. Why not live dangerously, and work out your answer before peeking? Take your time—we're going to propose a break in a couple of pages.

Answers for page 47:

Some of the descriptive attributes you might have listed could have been:

patients between the ages of 21 and 35

male patients

patients in the same building, floor or ward

Some of the behavioral attributes you listed might have been:

patients who fit #1 above, and who have made considerable progress while in the hospital (potential role models)

patients who have demonstrated a willingness to speak their minds, yet have shown consideration for the opinions of others and are able to dispel tension in group discussion

patients who have frequently discussed discharge with their fellow patients, but have been reluctant to do so with their caseworker on a one-to-one basis

patients discharged within 6 months to a year who are now holding a job successfully while residing outside the institution

If you listed anything like the attributes above, you've done some good thinking! This was a tough question. (*Note:* Both descriptive and behavioral attributes are useful here. The descriptive attributes mentioned might be characteristic of all potential members, e.g., two-three months from discharge. There might, however, be considerable differences in the behavioral attributes, e.g., ability to show consideration for the opinions of others.)

Answer for page 46:

B (note group objective)

AN EXCEPTION TO THE HOMOGENEOUS/HETEROGENEOUS RULE

In creating a group, our rule of thumb has been: 1) homogeneous descriptive attributes; 2) heterogeneous behavioral attributes. While this is a pretty good rule it may not apply if the *objective* for the group requires that the group be heterogeneous on descriptive attributes.

Example: Men *and* women in a group whose objective is to improve heterosexual relationships.

Example: Staff *and* clients in a group whose objective is to improve an agency's delivery of service to clients.

Example: A *diverse community committee* whose objective is to define and work on the improvement of community problems.

Note that groups that are heterogeneous on critical descriptive attributes will need to pay particular attention to problems of *communication* that would not exist if the members were homogeneous on critical descriptive attributes. This happens because individuals with significantly different descriptive attributes are likely to have different language patterns, different values, and a lack of common knowledge. For this reason, you cannot take for granted that individuals understand one another. Instead, you should encourage them to continually check out their understanding of one another's communication, both verbal and nonverbal.

Section 8

BEHAVIORALLY SPECIFIC OBJECTIVES

BEHAVIORALLY SPECIFIC OBJECTIVES

Before we turn to other things affecting composition,
let's pause awhile to talk about a basic supposition.

We've said that group objectives are the bases for deciding
which attributes are critical and therefore overriding.

But what we haven't done thus far is teach you how to write
a statement of objectives that's spe-ci-fically right.

So using Mager[6] as our guide, enriched by some examples,
we'll teach you how to write them right: below is our first
sample (and our last attempt at rhyming).

1. Given
   Given a group of six patients in a mental hospital who are to be
   discharged within the next three months,

2. Behavior
   each should be able to describe plans for their activities following
   discharge as regards family relationships, job, school, etc., That they
   have developed,

3. Criteria
   which, in the opinion of the group and the Group Worker would make
   it unnecessary for any group member to return to the hospital.

Given refers to:

the conditions under which the desired behavior will occur (our
sample: being in a group. We could have also selected our

"givens" in terms of circumstances outside of the group, e.g., once back in the community, following discharge . . . etc.).

Behavior refers to:

the desired behavior stated in terms of what people will be able to do; *not how they think or feel* (develop a plan for what they will do following discharge).

Criteria refers to:

the standards by which results are to be measured (group and Group Worker opinions that the plan will help the person avoid rehospitalization).

For each of the objectives stated below, indicate whether "Givens," "Behaviors," and "Criteria" are:

Specific   S

Non-specific   N

Absent   A

	Givens	Behavior	Criteria
Objective #1			
Objective #2			
Objective #3			

Objective #1:   When confronted with an opportunity to eat forbidden food, girls who are members of a group in a home for unwed mothers will have a good understanding of the dangers to themselves and their babies.

Objective #2:   The objective of the group was to teach the boys to express their anger constructively.

Objective #3:   When presented with any situation in which they could violate the law, each member of the gang voluntarily would act according to law in a majority of cases.

	Givens	Behavior	Criteria
Objective #1	S (You know the condition under which they are to act)	A (But what will they *do* with their "under-standing"?)	A (How well should they be able to do whatever they should be able to do?)
Objective #2	A (Under what con-ditions should they be able to express anger? #2 doesn't say)	N (Express their anger—verbally? through dramatic play? This needs greater specificity)	A (No standard for measuring this expres-sion—what is "constructive" expression of anger?)
Objective #3	S (Potential law violating situation)	S (act legally depending on the situation, e.g., when driv-ing, stay within the speed limit, etc.)	S (do so volun-tarily in a majority of cases)

Let's see if this is clear. Try rewriting Objectives #1 & 2 so that they *are* specific.

Objective #1: (In Objective #1, the Givens are satisfactory, so start with Behavior)

Objective #2: Rewrite "Givens" "Behavior" "Criteria"

Then compare them with our statements on the next page.

Objective #1:

　When confronted with an opportunity to eat forbidden food, girls who are members of a group in a home for unwed mothers will voluntarily choose to conform to doctor's orders in every single instance.

Objective #2:

　Given a social situation in which each boy had previously handled his anger dysfunctionally (in the opinion of others or of himself) he will be able to express this anger verbally to the person involved in such a way that that person would, if asked, be able to describe accurately the boy's reasons for being angry (as judged by the boy), and respond without counter-hostility, so that the issue between them is resolved to the satisfaction of each.

Now you try, from scratch. Assume that you want to write objectives for a group of senior citizens, living at home, who participate in the community center's Golden Age Club.

For example: (we'll start you with one of ours)

　　Objective:　　Given the fact that members are physically capable of leaving their homes without help, members should spend one evening a week in a social activity with one or more non-club members, away from the member's residence.

O.K. Try making one up for a group you now work with, or one you participate in socially.

　　Objective:　　?

　Rather than trying to second guess your choice, we'll refer you to our three variables. Rate your own objective and, where necessary (because it's non-specific or just not there) correct it.

　1. Given: are the conditions of performance specific? (Where?) (When?) (Who?)

2. Behaviors: have you talked in terms of observable behaviors? (Which?)

3. Criteria: do you have a standard by which to measure performance, and some way to apply this standard? (How well?) (How much?)

In addition, group development is more likely to occur when objectives meet the following criteria:

Clear | 1) the objectives must be clear to the potential member

Optional | 2) the potential member must have some choice in the selection of objectives and some power to create objectives.

Possible | 3) the potential member must believe the objectives are possible to achieve.

Beneficial | 4) the achievement of the objectives should include beneficial outcomes for each individual member.

SUMMARY

Clarity of group objective makes it possible to deal with a number of other issues, when creating or modifying a group. Now, we're going to list these issues, to let you see what you have coming. After you've read this page, we suggest you take a break.

1) the *choice* individuals should have about themselves or others becoming group members; and the choice members have in selecting group objectives;

2) the need for a *reservoir* (or pool) of individuals from which potential members can be nominated, and

3) how much *influence* the Group Worker should have with regard to establishing the reservoir and nomination of group members;

4) the kind of *environment* (or setting) you need to facilitate group development;

5) the length of *time* the group should meet;

6) the appropriate *number* of members for a particular group.

Ready for a break? Take five . . . see you on page 57, whenever you're ready.

NOTE

6. Robert F. Mager, Developing Instructional Objectives, op. cit.

Section 9

FIVE IMPORTANT CONSIDERATIONS IN GROUP CREATION

A. *CHOICE*—TO JOIN OR NOT TO JOIN—THAT IS THE QUESTION!

Many social work clients receive service on a quasi-voluntary basis; i.e., they have comparatively little choice about joining the group. For example: psychiatric hospital patients are expected to participate in a discharge planning group; a youngster is brought to a child guidance clinic by his mother; a welfare mother is strongly "encouraged" by her caseworker to attend a group whose purpose is to orient her toward seeking employment. You can probably think of others.

For example: (your turn)

Effective groups are groups in which members like to be. Can a group be effective if some members don't want to be in it? Unfortunately there are no pat answers to this question, but when an involuntary member enters a group, he is more likely to come to like it if he sees others liking it. On the other hand a potential member is more likely to use a group experience effectively when he or she is *clear* about how the group operates, considers the purpose of the group to be *important* to him or her and considers the objective to be *achievable*. The individual's decision to join or not join the group can be viewed as a critical attribute. In order to increase the knowledge of a potential member so that he or she will be able to make an informed decision, you may want to provide an opportunity to observe the group in action by:

visiting a group meeting

listening to an audio tape of a group meeting

reading a transcript of a group meeting

viewing a video tape of a group meeting.

Of the two examples given below,

1. In which did individuals have a choice about joining? _____

2. In which was there no choice? _____

A	B
Six young adults, seated in the waiting room of the Employment Service were told to go to a nearby room, where they would be given a chance to learn something about the counseling process they were about to enter.	Six youngsters in a junior high class who were in academic trouble were invited to join a group that was being formed to help students learn how to manage their classroom experiences more effectively.

3. Do you have enough information to predict which is more
likely to become an effective group?   Yes_____ No _____

Many factors go into making a group "effective." What you
might say is: the more members who want to join a group, the
more likely it will become an effective group—quickly. Therefore:

1. The degree of choice a member feels he or she has about joining a group
   is influenced by the degree of choice he or she has in determining group
   objectives.

2. Determining the nominee's attitude toward entering a group requires
   talking with him or her before the group begins.

3. In the same vein, members may feel more positively toward a group in
   which they can exercise some choice about new members entering the
   group.

4. Finally, members should know who the Group Worker is going to
   be so that they can take that into account when they make their
   decision about joining the group.

Now, let's consider the agency. An agency must have a reservoir of potential members in order to allow both Group Worker choice and member choice in determining group membership.

B. A *RESERVOIR* OF POTENTIAL CLIENTS AND THE GROUP WORKER'S INFLUENCE IN THE NOMINATION OF POTENTIAL GROUP MEMBERS

Since agency conditions vary considerably, you have to balance the following guidelines with the steps that are feasible in your setting. The *more you depart* from these guidelines, the *less you can expect* to use group composition as a way of affecting the achievement of group objectives.

GUIDELINES

A. Reservoir—there should be a reservoir of individuals from which to nominate potential members.

B. Influence—the Group Worker should play a major role in determining who is to be nominated and selected for group membership.

C. Access—the Group Worker should have direct access to the reservoir of potential members.

D. Critical Attributes—where the Group Worker cannot have direct access to a reservoir of potential members because referral is the appropriate procedure, the Group Worker should inform all referring agents of the critical attributes for this particular group.

Which of the guidelines have been followed in each of the situations below?

1. The Principal and the Social Worker agreed that a group for 6th-grade boys who were failing two or more courses could be useful. The Principal agreed to the Worker's suggestion that the group have six to eight members and that both withdrawn

Answers for page 58:

1. B; 2. A; 3. If you said "no" you're right; group A, for example, might happen to contain a better balance of behavioral attributes than is found in B. You may be asking: is "desire to join" a behavioral attribute? Yes, it is. Then, you may ask, do we want heterogeneity on this behavioral attribute a la pages 23-38? This is a complicated issue: in this case, we need *at least* a balance, if not a preponderance of "desire to join." As on page 50, Group Objective sometimes overrules our homogeneity/heterogeneity guideline.

and disruptive boys be included. The Principal then contacted the three 6th-grade teachers and asked each to give him the names of two or three boys who were failing two or more courses. Eventually, he sent the names of seven boys to the Worker.

A. Reservoir _____   B. Influence _____
           Yes/No   Yes/No

C. Access _____   D. Attributes _____
           Yes/No   Yes/No

2. Although the public welfare caseworkers expressed interest in group work service for their clients, referrals were not forthcoming. The Group Worker had been hired to introduce group work services to the agency. To acquaint him with the agency's operation, he had been assigned a small caseload. He had told the caseworkers that the group's purpose would be to assist welfare mothers in solving problems of raising children when the children's father was not living at home. In order to avoid administrative hassling, the Group Worker had discussed the group with several caseworkers, on an individual basis, but had not talked about it with any supervisor.

A. Reservoir _____   B. Influence _____
                   Yes/No   Yes/No

C. Access _____   D. Attributes _____
                Yes/No   Yes/No

(answers on page 62)

But what can you do to avoid a situation in which the Principal sends only seven names when you want a reservoir of, say twelve, from which to select?

1) You ask him to add more names so that you can form the most effective group, suggesting a minimum number.

In the public welfare setting, what might you do to avoid the caseworkers' predictable resistance to making referrals?

One answer: clear first with the supervisors, so as to have greater influence; state critical attributes in greater detail.

A different answer: Get your own caseload, and then develop a demonstration group from your caseload. Once the demonstration group has been shown to be effective, approach the supervisors, etc.

In light of what has been said with regard to "Reservoir and "Influence" what is missing from each of the following?

1. The Group Worker asked the nurses on the psychiatric ward to send men to his group who need to develop improved social skills.

2. The Juvenile Court workers were told by their supervisor to refer any of their clients who they thought might benefit from group services.

3. The psychiatrist at the clinic listed five of his patients who were "having trouble with peer relationships" and asked the group worker to work with them as a group.

Answers for pages 60 and 61:

1. A, No; B, No; C, No; D, Yes.   2. A, No; B, No; C, No;
   D, No.

While each answer may be different in specifics, we think the three examples share common pitfalls,. Reliance on others to make referrals usually leads to no referrals, unless some supporting administrative procedures are developed to insure that referrals will come. Such procedures must include the development of a reservoir of potential clients, and ways to maximize the Group Worker's influence over the administrative aspects of group creation.

Incidentally, the fact that group objective was extremely vague in all of the examples was a factor that complicated the problems discussed above. Without a clear set of objectives neither the Group Worker nor the referral agents can develop a potential reservoir of clients. In the next section, we'll discuss "Environment" (or setting).

C. ENVIRONMENT

It is amazing to us that people continually overlook the effect of a group's immediate environment on interaction. For example:

Miss G., a group work student, was assigned to work with a group of six students who were in a special education class for drop-outs. Participation in this class was supposed to facilitate job placement but attendance was spotty, the teacher's motivation poor and class morale low. Miss G. was expected to meet with her group in the back of the classroom, behind a free standing, lightly constructed screen. As can be imagined, the noise of classroom activities proved distracting; in addition, group members were denied privacy and were therefore unwilling to discuss concerns. The class was an overflow program from the high school, and met in space rented within another building. Two fair sized rooms, directly across the hall, were unoccupied, but were locked and unavailable to the program. The classroom setting proved to be a major stumbling block in relation to the group's development.

There are a great many variables to be considered with regard to environment, e.g., size of meeting room, arrangement of chairs, place to meet (home, car, agency lounge, etc.), privacy, location of meeting place and ease of reaching it, and so forth. Basically, however, choice of setting should be guided by two considerations, both of which relate to objective:

1. **Evidence of preplanning**: Most people like to know that some consideration has been given to their comfort. Meeting at a time that is convenient for all, having ash trays for smokers, being able to shut a door to insure privacy, having coffee available when members arrive, etc., are all indications to clients that the Group Worker cares enough about them to have prepared for them.

2. **Atmosphere**: The situation in which a group of people find themselves has a definite effect on the mood of the group. A small room can provide a feeling of intimacy for one group or a feeling of crowding for another. For some groups, meeting in a station wagon can provide an exciting, attractive setting, and so forth.

In which of the examples did the Group Worker give members evidence of preplanning for the meeting?

A	B
The Group Worker arrived to find the room set up for a class—rows of chairs facing a desk. He moved the chairs into a circle, laid copies of the agenda the group had selected on each chair, set out ash trays around the floor and put out name tags for each member on the table.	The Group Worker called each member to make sure that they had transportation to the meeting. He arrived a few minutes early with the motion picture projector and film the group had said they wanted to see. He found the room locked, and by the time the maintenance man came to open it, several members had arrived. They found the room a mess—the maintenance man had gotten in-

	volved in a plumbing emergency and had forgotten to get things ready.

Neither _____ Both _____ A. _____ B. _____

In which of the examples did the Worker set a good atmosphere for the group meeting?

A	B
The boys had agreed to spend the first half hour planning their trip, and then go to the gym for the kind of active games they loved. To save time, the Group Worker decided to spend the first thirty minutes in a corner of the gym, then to break into games. When they arrived, they found gym equipment readily at hand and the boys began to toss the basketballs around.	The Group Worker had several decks of cards on the tables so that as the men arrived, they started playing. Several helped themselves to the coffee and doughnuts that had been prepared for them. When everyone had arrived, the Worker asked the men to leave the card games and join him over in the corner of the room. The men came quietly in ones and twos, pulled the sofas together, and sat down, ready to begin.

Both _____ Neither _____ A. _____ B. _____

Answer for top of page 64:

A. (He tried in B, but as far as the members were concerned, he hadn't tried hard enough.)

Answer for bottom of page 64:

B   (re A: serious planning and basketball don't mix . . .)

D. TIME

Some groups need only meet once to accomplish their objective effectively. One good example of this would be a meeting which orients new clients to the range of service offered by an agency. Other groups require a considerable amount of time and many meetings to accomplish their objective. For example: A social worker maintained active contact with a delinquent gang group for two years before antisocial behavior decreased enough to terminate his contact with the members of the group. Further, some groups are time-limited while others are "open" in terms of the time that individuals stay in the group as well as the life of the group itself.

Of the two examples below,

1. Which is time-limited? _____

2. Which is open? _____

A	B
Four married couples met for twelve weeks to discuss marital problems with a Family Service Worker. At the end of that time (by prior agreement) the group ended. Members were free to join a new group, seek individual counseling, or terminate contact with the agency.	All girls approaching termination were moved to a "discharge cottage" in an institution for delinquent girls. For about six weeks before leaving they participated in a group whose purpose was to prepare them for discharge. As one member left the institution, a new member was added to the cottage. The discharge group continued but its membership changed continually. Also, some girls who needed it stayed longer than six weeks in the cottage.

(Answers on page 68.)

There is no optimum length of time for *all* groups. Optimal group duration is determined by group objective. In fact, research in psycotherapy indicates that when the therapist expects treatment will take about two years for treatment goals to be achieved, it usually takes that long, whereas if he or she really expects that only three months will be needed, three months often prove sufficient.[7] In short, be optimistic about the time needed. The reality of time limits helps groups to develop quickly.

Similarly, groups are more likely to be effective if the Group Worker (or the Group Worker together with the group) has "worked" out decisions about meeting frequency, length of meetings and time of meetings, than if the traditional, "50-minute-hour-once-a-week" is used automatically. This is particularly important where the Group Worker and clients may have different ideas about time, how it should be organized, used, etc.

> Example: Four boys were about to be expelled from a junior high school. Because of this impending crisis, the school Social Worker arranged to meet with them three times a week, during school hours, for four weeks.
>
> Meetings were held during luncheon hour—a point about mid-way in the school day. The time-limited nature of the group was explained in terms of group objective: to provide a "last chance," with little time for "horsing around."
>
> The boys accepted the realities of the situation and immediately got down to business.

Suppose that you're a social work student placed in a Juvenile Court, and that you are planning a treatment group for parents of boys returning from placement in a correctional institution. The objective of the group *is to enable the parents to provide appropriate support and "parenting" to prevent a recurrence of their sons' antisocial behaviors.* Please use the following list of time considerations to decide how you would use time to develop an effective parents group. (You can assume, for purposes of this question, that you have appropriate *influence* over matters pertaining to this group's formation, e.g., reservoir, etc.)

Time considerations in group creation
(Please answer by writing your responses after each question.)

1. How long should the meeting last?

2. When do you think it would be best to hold the first group meeting?

3. How often should the group meet?

4. At what time of the day should the group meet?

5. Should there be a time limit for the "life" of the group?

6. Should the group meet at the same time, each time?

7. Does the fact that time is viewed differently by different cultural groups have any relevance to planning for this group?

You might have listed things like:

1. _____ Hold meetings to a maximum of 1-1/2 hours so that the parents don't get "talked out," and will retain focus on providing support and improved parenting to their sons.

2. _____ Bring parents into the group at least one month prior to the boys' release so that the group can help the parents plan for the actual return of each boy to his home.

3. _____ Once a week may be all most parents can manage: the group might want to increase this just before or after "release" occurs, to provide support to members as they prepare for their sons' return.

4. _____ Evening meetings so that both parents can be present, since the group's objective pertains to both parents.

5. _____ Establish a time limit (such as three months after discharge), but keep it open so that new parents can join about one month before their boy is discharged, while "old parents" help "new" ones over the hurdles; at this time, the group will be reconstituted, continued, or terminated.

6. _____ Meeting at the same time helps to establish good attendance habits, which helps the group to develop so that members can work together to achieve the group's objective.

7. _____ This will depend on what you can find out about the parents and the community. If your answer to #7 conflicts with your response to #6, you should give priority to your #7 answer in working out time arrangements.

E. NUMBER

Research shows that as groups get larger: participation decreases; satisfaction decreases; consensus decreases; leadership requirements increase; intimacy among members decreases; and subgroups emerge.[8] On the other hand, as groups get larger, they are able to tackle more complex tasks. It's interesting to note that it's been found that as size increases there is an increase in tension release, giving suggestions, and asking opinions of others. In addition, it's been found that groups of four and six show more disagreement and antagonism than do groups of three, five, or seven, and that members ask for suggestions less in the even-numbered groups.

There is no optimum size; there are no set rules about size. Ideally, each group must be created (with regard to size) in terms of the objective of the group and the attributes of its members. Extremely disturbed individuals may need a smaller group (three or four) so as not to be "lost" as they might be in a larger group. A patient government group might need to be larger (ten-twelve) in order to be representative as well as capable of coping with complex problems.

Most groups are composed of individuals who are likely to interact in negative ways from time to time. It would appear that some degree of conflict is inevitable *and potentially useful.* This suggests that the group should not be too small, e.g., three, or too large, e.g., fifteen, if a *tolerable* amount of useful stress is to develop. At the same time there should be enough people to interact with regard to resolving problems that are conflictual.

NOTES

7. Arnold P. Goldstein. *Therapist-Patient Expectations in Psychotherapy*, N.Y.; The MacMillan Co., 1962. pp. 76-85.

8. Edwin J. Thomas and Clinton F. Fink, "Effects of Group Size," *Psychological Bulletin*, 1963, 60, 371-384.

REVIEW

OBSERVATIONS ABOUT GROUPS

(A) The larger the group, the less focus on individual members.

> *Good* if you want people to have an opportunity to gradually move into active participation without immediate demands placed on them.
>
> *Not Good* if you want to quickly establish that the group is designed to provide maximum benefit for each member, and you think individuals can and should be involved quickly.

(B) The larger the group, the less damage will be done to group morale if some members are absent or drop out.

(C) The larger the group, the more complex program planning can be; on the other hand the easier it is for individual members to get "lost," unattended to, misunderstood or not helped by the group experience.

(D) The larger the group the more members are required to share the attention of the Group Worker.

Good in the sense that this requires them to turn to one another for help.

Not Good if they panic in a group without the immediate support of the Group Worker and/or are very jealous of the attention given to other members by the Group Worker.

Three treatment groups are described below; in each case, use the following symbols to indicate whether you think the group's size is:

"+" for "too large"

"√" for "about right"

"−" for "too small."

The gang numbered 25 members. However, many members participated infrequently.

The Group Worker selected the nine most faithful members of the gang and offered to create a treatment group for them. (Please judge the size of this core group.)

This group seems to be _____ .

Three children ages seven-eight were each experiencing severe difficulties in peer relationships within a cottage group of ten.

To help them develop better friendships in the cottage, the Group Worker created a time-limited group of five children from the cottage including the above three plus two children who were particularly popular with the other kids.

This group seems to be _____ .

A three-session-in-one-week orientation group for new girls (in a home for unwed mothers) was created to help girls with problems of entering the program and learning about its resources;

One week fourteen girls entered the Home. The Group Worker decided to work with the week's new girls as a group.

This group seems to be _____ .

(Answers on page 74.)

Answers and rationale for pages 72 and 73:

____√____ (about right)

> Twenty-five was clearly unmanageable in terms of effective contact between the Group Worker and individual members.
>
> Hopefully, frequent, intensive contact with the nine could influence the other gang members.

____√____ (about right)

> This group was sufficiently small that much attention could be given the three, but not so small, or so composed that it appeared as a disciplinary group for "bad kids."
>
> The addition of the two popular kids served a useful function, but more than these two could have left the initial three out in the cold.

____+____ (too many)

> The orientation group was designed to impart information—information which is often best secured through questions raised by a number of different members.
>
> Large size, in this instance, might have caused several people to remain silent, even though they had important questions.
>
> It might have been better to split the group in half and meet separately with two distinct groups.

Now let's review. To date, we have indicated a number of key factors that should be attended to when creating a group. For reasons that may be obvious, these are presented below in a slightly different order than you found them in the program.

C	*Choice*	The degree to which the member chooses to be in the group should be noted as a significant behavioral attribute; further, potential members should participate in choosing group members as much as possible.
R	*Reservoir*	The Group Worker should attempt to develop a reservoir (or pool) of potential members.
E	*Environment*	The group's immediate environment (or setting) should be planned and designed so that the resulting group atmosphere enhances group effectiveness.
A	*Attributes*	The group members should be homogeneous with respect to descriptive attributes, and heterogeneous with respect to behavioral attributes.
T	*Time*	The Group Worker should make maximum use of planned time to enhance group effectiveness.
I	*Influence*	The Group Worker should be able to influence decisions about the selection of group members.
O	*Objective*	The Group Worker's objective for the group should be explicit because *it serves as the basis for most decisions and planning with regard to group creation.*
N	*Numbers*	Group size should be determined so that it will enhance group effectiveness.

Perhaps the trick of remembering a variety of associated ideas through the use of a key word is "old hat" but (as you have probably already noticed) the first letters of the key words above spell "CREATION." Hopefully, this acronym will help you to recall significant factors that are involved in group creation.

THE ATTRIBUTES OF THE WORKER

We would like to conclude the review of the material on group creation by commenting on one additional factor in the process, and then by summing up the process with both a flow chart and an outline as aids for composing a group. Thus far we have not considered the attributes of the Group Worker him/herself. Let's discuss this vital factor for a moment.

Experience has demonstrated that some Group Workers prefer and/or are better (than other workers) with children, senior citizens, hospital patients, or some other group-type within the population. On the other hand, certain individuals may initially experience greater comfort with (and thus be more willing to be influenced by) a Group Worker who is similar to them with regard to age, sex, race, religion, etc. Although the Group Worker is not a member of the group, he or she is a central person in the group; therefore, all of the considerations about group creation that we have presented so far have pertinence for matching the Worker with the group.

We would like you to think about the most significant factors from the CREATION list on the previous page as they relate to assignment of a group worker to a group. For example:

1) Should clients have the choice of one Group Worker from a reservoir of Workers?

2) Should Group Workers have a choice of serving one out of several groups after they have been created?

3) Should a Group Worker's descriptive attributes be as close to those of the group members as possible with regards to such things as age, sex, race, etc.?

4) Should more than one Group Worker be assigned to a group to provide such things as a variety of worker-models, a variety of worker behavioral attributes, etc.?

Clearly, answers to these questions would require a separate program in itself. We can only suggest that you use what has been covered up to this point to answer questions like these about the assignment of Group Worker(s) to a group.

Now turn to the flow chart. After looking it over carefully, please move to the problem that follows it.

Section 11

GROUP COMPOSITION FLOW CHART AND OUTLINE

Given a clear articulation at agency goals; the Group Worker will follow the action path shown in the flow chart below:

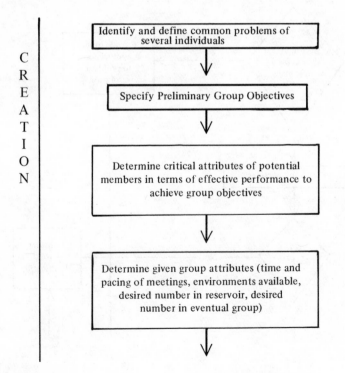

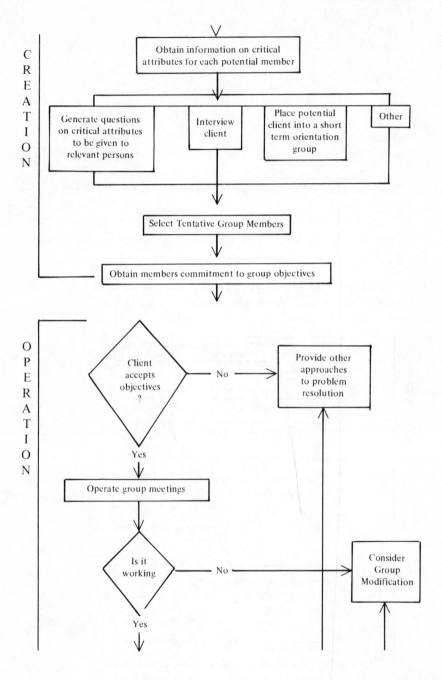

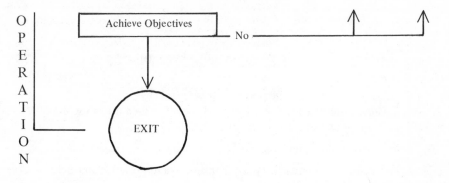

The outline below is intended to clarify the flow chart and assist workers in the step by step process of Group Creation. Given a clear articulation of agency goals:

1) What are common problems of clients that could be addressed through group work?

2) Assuming you have decided to attempt a group approach to the resolution of certain common problems what would be your preliminary *objectives* for such a group? (These objectives would be renegotiated with the group members once the group has begun to meet.)

   A. Under the following conditions . . .
   B. Members should be able to . . .
   C. According to the following criteria . . .

3) Based on the preliminary objectives for the group, critical *attributes* would be:

   A. Descriptive
   B. Behavioral (include ability and experience)

4) At this point in time, what plans would you make concerning:

   A. *Influence* (What do you have to do to create optimum conditions within the agency for this group, e.g., with whom do you have to clear the idea, etc.?)
   B. *Reservoir* (How large do you want it to be; how can you insure sufficient numbers?)
   C. *Environment* (Meeting where, etc.?)
   D. *Time* (Starting when, running how long, meeting how often, how long and at what time of day, etc.?)
   E. *Number* (How large do you want the group to be?)
   F. *Choice* (Degree and nature of choice about joining?)

5) How will you obtain information about critical attributes for each potential member?

    A. Generate specific questions for information gathering by

    1. Referral agent

    2. Yourself (interviewing potential member).

    B. Show potential members a sample meeting, then interview them.

    C. Invite potential member to an orientation group.

6) Compare data on behavioral attributes to achieve a workable balance,

7) Select potential members, using descriptive and (balance of) behavioral attributes.

8) Determine how will you notify potential members that they have been selected?

9) Develop plans for potential members who were told about the group but not selected?

Section 12

GROUP CREATION–A PROBLEM

The following case material is presented to enable you to test out what you have learned from this program. Acceptable performance means that you have achieved the first Instructional Objective, as described on page 9. Why not look at page 9 before proceeding, then return to the following paragraph.

Now, here are some vital pieces of information about a number of boys who are potential members of a group to be sponsored by the Juvenile Court. Using the outline just presented, *create the most effective treatment group possible.* Also, state what further information you would like to have and why you want it.

Given:

1) fifteen potential clients.

2) all of the boys described below either are on or were on probation for several acts of breaking and entering, property damage, or other violations. They will probably be placed in correctional institutions for any recurrence of law violation if it occurs after their seventeenth birthday.

GROUP OBJECTIVES

Once members have terminated from this group, they will no longer engage in illegal behavior, so that institutional placements will not be necessary for any of them. In addition, they will develop and act on prosocial goals for themselves, e.g., return to and maintain satisfactory performance in school, become involved in training for employment, seeking, securing and holding a job, etc., and will work consistently to achieve their goal(s).

Rationale: The purpose of a Juvenile Court with regard to juveniles who are adjudicated delinquent, is to see to it that those juveniles who violate the law do not continue to do so. We assume that law-abiding behavior is more likely to occur if the individual is "making it" in society in some legally acceptable way. Accordingly, the group objective must include both restraining aspects (no further law violation) and facilitating aspects (working to achieve prosocial goals).

Where no mention of probation status is made, you can assume the boy is still on probation.

1. *DONALD W.* (Age 14)—8th grade—Black. Interests—pets. Lower-lower class. Below average intelligence. Docile, uninvolved in any ongoing activity. No previous group or institutional experience. Little interest in socializing, a "lone wolf." *With gang in breaking and entering.*

2. *ROBERT T.* (Age 16)—10th grade—Black. Interests—mechanical work. Lower class. Average intelligence. Spent six months in Boys Training School with group experience. Aggressive, domineering, hostile. Loud voice, compulsive talker, pushes own ideas in group but doesn't take responsibility for follow through on own ideas. *Broke probation, which was based upon mother's statement that he was out of her control.*

3. *RAY D.* (Age 16)—10th grade—White. Now living in detention home. Interests—chemistry, athletics. Low middle-class family. Well above average intelligence. No previous group work or institutional experience. Independent, somewhat aloof from peers and adults. Seems to be afraid of getting too close to anyone, won't talk in social groups, remains uninvolved when group takes action. *Stealing cars and reckless driving; incorrigible according to parents.*

4. *GENE R.* (Age 15)—9th grade—Black. Interests—does good school work; likes fighting, exciting activities. Lower class. High intelligence. Spent eight months in detention home. No group work experience. Leader of delinquent gang. Effective at controlling

group, but not physical aggression; rather is good at effecting compromises; has a good sense of humor. Has been off probation for several months, doing well in an auto mechanics training school. *Breaking and entering.*

5. *GEORGE D.* (Age 16)—10th grade—White. Interests—athletics, cars. Lower-middle class. Above average intelligence. No previous group work or institutional experience. Conforming, a follower. Can become very verbal when cars are discussed, otherwise rarely opens his mouth. *Several drinking violations—drunk and disorderly in public.* Is not now on probation.

6. *JOHN V.* (Age 16)—10th grade—Black. Interests—track, football. Lower class. Average intelligence. Participated in group work program at Community Center—noninstitutional experience. Blows up, falls apart when frustrated. Gene R.'s friend, sometimes follows Gene into trouble. Gene plays an important role in helping John to control his temper. *Breaking and entering.*

7. *JIM S.* (Age 15)—9th grade—Black. Interests—biology and track. Lower class. Above average intelligence. No previous group or institutional experience. Subtle leader, skillful manipulator, the "cool" type. Distrustful of adults so that he operates behind the scenes; particularly dislikes social workers but, in their presence, appears to be a conformist. *Stealing.* Off probation, doing passing work in school.

8. *JERRY M.* (Age 15)—10th grade—White. Interests—hunting, fishing. Lower class. Average intelligence. No previous group work or institutional experience. Very aggressive; assaulted father twice with hammer, although provoked each time. Uncomfortable in the presence of Blacks. Hot temper—fears he will lose it so avoids group contacts. Has occasionally been led into trouble by one adult. *Assault with weapon (father).*

9. *GEORGE A.* (Age 16)—Out of school—White. Interests—metal work, welding. Lower class. Below average intelligence. Eliminated from a previous group work experience because of aggressive behavior. Breaks rules, acts as a "know it all." Backs down when confronted by forceful person. *Chronic truancy.*

10. *ROBERT B.* (Age 15)—Out of school—White. Interests—cars. Lower class. Below average intelligence. Unemployed, deemed "uneducable." Docile, quiet, meek. Will follow any leader. *Stealing.*

11. *JOE F.* (Age 16)—11th grade—Black. Interests—music (drums). Lower class. Above average intelligence. No group work or institutional

experience. Follower—small boy, docile. Music teacher indicates he has exceptional talent but Joe is afraid to try for fear he will fail; others like him because of his musical ability and the fact that he poses no threat. *Stealing.*

12. *PETE S.* (Age 16)—Out of school—Black. Unemployed. Interests— cars. Lower class. Below average intelligence. One year in Boys Training School. No group work experience. Aggressive, huge; takes over. Clumsy—covers his embarrassment at being awkward by a "don't care" manner. *Several breaking and enterings and car thefts.*

13. *RALPH O.* (Age 17)—9th grade—Black. Interests—sports, gang activity. Lower class. Average ability. Poor school performance, reading problem. No previous group work or institutional experience. Involved in gang fights. Witty, quick in remarks. Verbally cuts others down. Close friend of Gene R's, but doesn't always follow Gene's lead. *Gang activity—destruction of property.*

14. *WILLIAM C.* (Age 16)—10th grade—White. Interests—carpentry, woodworking. Lower middle class. Above average ability. In Boys Training School six months. Quiet, a loner, can be angered if teased; spends most of his time with one girl. Does not want to be in a group. *Two breaking and enterings.*

15. *STAN W.* (Age 16)—10th Grade—White. Interests—football, basketball. Middle class. Superior ability, poor school performance; no previous group work experience. Plays it smart, wise, initiates action. Pseudo-sophisticated; aggressive, tense and nervous; always on the go; excitement seeker. In previous social contacts has been seen as initiator of antisocial behavior. *Drunk and disorderly.*

The solution that follows is one that makes sense to us. Undoubtedly, there are other possible groupings. Essentially, this program has attempted to teach an approach to group creation that should prove useful to the practitioner. It will be up to you, the reader, to decide whether or not it has been helpful. Incidentally, we view this problem as a good focal point for class discussion of problems associated with group creation. *But before you read our solution, work on yours.*

I. Common Problems

All of the boys described below either are on or were on probation for several acts of breaking and entering, property damage, or other violations. They will probably be placed in correctional institutions for any recurrence of law violation if it occurs after their seventeenth birthday.

II. *Group Objective* (Here is ours):

Once members have terminated from this group, they will no longer engage in illegal behavior, so that institutional placements will not be necessary for any of them. In addition, they will develop and act on prosocial goals for themselves, e.g., return to and maintain satisfactory performance in school, become involved in training for employment, seeking, securing and holding a job, etc., and will work consistently to achieve their goal(s).

III. *Critical Attributes*

  A. With regard to group purpose
    1. Descriptive attributes
       While it may appear unnecessary to say this, it is important to note that considerable selection has already preceded our actions in creating a group. Accordingly, all of the potential members share certain descriptive attributes:

       a. all are males
       b. all are adolescents (although a fourteen year old adolescent may be at a very different level of maturation than a sixteen year old)
       c. all are now (or have been) on probation
       d. all are likely candidates for placement in a correctional institution

       In our view, the above four factors represent critical descriptive attributes for this group. In our community, at this time, racial difference is a significant factor affecting peer interaction, so that "race" may be a critical attribute. Socio-economic class differences do not appear to be a significant factor to us for this group. (You might disagree.)
       Nature-of-offense might be of importance, e.g., nine boys have engaged in some kind of theft activity—stealing, breaking and entering, car theft—

which may be considerably different from truancy or alcoholism, but not, in our view, of sufficient importance to make the actual legal offense itself a critical attribute.

2. Behavioral Attributes

In only one instance (William C.) do we have any information about client voluntarism with regard to group treatment. Nevertheless, it seems to us that it would be important to know how each boy views the group objective of eliminating illegal behavior and at the same time "making it" in a prosocial way. Accordingly, we would establish client voluntarism as a critical behavioral attribute, with a goal of achieving some balance in the degree of voluntarism. If this information is not available, we might have to do without.

Since elimination of illegal behavior is a prime purpose of the group, a second critical attribute could relate to the degree to which the individual has previously been known to initiate illegal acts. Thus, we could establish the following continuum based on subjective assessment of available information:

History of Following Others Into Illegal Acts, Rather Than Initiating Them

Almost Never	Infrequently	Sometime	Frequently	Almost Always
1	2	3	4	5
4. Gene R.	2. Robert T.	6. John V.	(No One)	1. Donald W.
15. Stan W.	7. Jim S.	8. Jerry M.		3. Ray D.
	9. George A.	13. Ralph O.		5. George D.
	12. Pete S.			8. Jerry M.
				10. Robert B.
				11. Joe F.
				12. William C.

One is immediately struck by the number of boys who have been seen as "followers." While it would be premature to select or eliminate any boys at this stage, we should keep this continuum in mind when we eventually attempt to achieve a balance of behavioral attributes.

A third critical behavioral attribute relating to group purpose that we thought important relates to the interest, experiences and abilities individuals have that might be capitalized on in moving boys toward school or employment opportunities.

Demonstrates Possession of Pro-Social Interests and Skills Related to School and Work

Almost Never	Infrequent	Sometime	Frequent	Almost Always
1	2	3	4	5

13. Ralph O.	6. John V.	1. Donald W.	2. Robert T.	4. Gene R.
	8. Jerry M.	10. Robert B.	3. Ray D.	14. William C.
	15. Stan W.	12. Pete S.	5. George D.	
			7. Jim S.	
			9. George A.	
			11. Joe F.	

Again our information is inadequate—although typical of the kind of information most Group Workers have to work from—but it does appear that a number of the boys have interests and/or skills that could be useful in work and/or school.

B. With regard to group development

1. Descriptive Attributes

We said earlier that race is a major descriptive attribute in terms of the purpose of the group. Obviously were the purpose different, e.g., fostering "black pride," etc., then race would be even more critical. On the other hand, if many of the boys have strong negative feelings about associating with members of another race, the group's development would be hindered. While our information here is sparse, Jerry M. might be considered for membership only if the group turns out to be composed predominantly of white boys.

2. Behavioral Attributes

Task and socio-emotional ability, plus the ability to model prosocial behaviors appear to be critical behavioral attributes in this group, in relation to its development.

Has Been Observed to Perform Task Acts

Almost Never	Infrequently	Sometime	Frequently	Almost Always
1	2	3	4	5

1. Donald W.	5. George D.	4. Gene R.	2. Robert T.	(No One)
3. Ray D.	15. Stan W.	6. John V.	7. Jim S.	
8. Jerry M.			12. Pete S.	
9. George A.				
10. Robert B.				
11. Joe F.				
13. Ralph O.				
14. William C.				

Selection of appropriate models would be based on those particular attitudes and/or behaviors we would like to see imitated. In a sense, each continuum developed so far provides potential models and modelers, e.g., a boy who has particular interests and/or skills could model this behavior for those who have no such involvement, etc. However, there is one further critical attribute that we would like to add since it appears to be a serious deficit for some: the ability to control impulsive, antisocial behavior.

Has Been Observed to Perform Socio-Emotional Acts

Almost Never	Infrequently	Sometime	Frequently	Almost Always
1	2	3	4	5

1. Don W.	(No One)	(No One)	11. Joe F.	4. Gene R.
2. Robert T.				
3. Ray D.				
5. George D.				
6. John V.				
7. Jim S.				
8. Jerry S.				
9. George A.				
10. Robert B.				
12. Pete S.				
13. Ralph O.				
14. William C.				
15. Stan W.				

Has Been Observed to Control Own Impulsive, Anti-Social Behavior

Almost Never	Infrequently	Sometime	Frequently	Almost Always
1	2	3	4	5

6. John V.	2. Robert T.	1. Don W.	3. Ray D.	4. Gene R.
8. Jerry M.	5. George D.	11. Joe F. (?)	7. Jim S.	
9. George A.	10. Robert B.		15. Stan W.	
	12. Pete S.			
	13. Ralph O.			
	14. William C.			

IV.

    A. *Influence*

        Getting referrals may prove difficult in some courts. If this proved to be the case here, it might be best for one staff member to create this group from his or her caseload.

B. *Client Reservoir*

In this case, it is sufficiently large to allow for choice. Since we have decided to make this an open-ended group, some procedure would have to be worked out so that potential new boys could be referred routinely.

C. *Environment*

For many juveniles, the setting of a Juvenile Court is not conducive to the kinds of relaxation that might prove necessary for boys to share concerns comfortably in the group. In our city, there is a community center located four blocks away from the County Court House. It is centrally located, and thus easily accessible by car or bus. The Center's program is flexible enough for us to use the building, e.g., rearrange furniture, serve refreshments, etc. Accordingly, we would plan to meet at the Center.

D. *Time*

Ten of the fifteen boys are sixteen years of age or older. It was stated that if they break the law once they are seventeen, they will be placed in an institution. Since it is the purpose of the group to avoid the necessity for such a placement, short duration (three to six months) might be appropriate. On the other hand, it could be useful to make this an "open-ended" group, i.e., one in which new members are added as old members leave, because of the prosocial modeling that the remaining "older" members could provide for newer members. Accordingly, each boy could be told that he would be expected to "graduate" in three to six months, with the understanding that as members leave, new members would be added. (Graduates could retain a quasi-official membership and be involved as helpers.)

Incidentally, note that the given age for the boys, e.g., "sixteen" is quite nonspecific. Are they all just about to turn seventeen? Did they just become six-teen? In other words, age might prove to be a critical attribute. If so, you would need to have birth dates for purposes of decision-making.

E. *Number*

While groups of six to eight appear to be preferred by many group workers (small enough to allow for individualization, large enough to remain a group in spite of absent members), such a group automatically eliminates nine (or seven) other individuals. It is possible that two groups could be created. It is also possible that several of the boys would profit more from a one-to-one contact.

F. *Choice*

Membership in this group could be made a condition of probation. However, it's probably best to ask the boys how they would feel about such a group before making this decision.

V. Obtaining Information

This was not specified in the information you were given. In working out the procedure referred to above, it would be essential to indicate critical attributes, so that boys for the group who would be inappropriate would not be referred only to be turned away.

VI. Compare Data: Behavioral Attributes

Each of the attributes is stated in relation to the absence or presence of prosocial behavior, e.g. with "absence" at the *low* end of the continuum, assigned a score of "1", etc.

Averaging the ratings each boy received on the five critical behavioral attributes produces the following table:

Names	Illegal Acts	Interest and Skills	Task Acts	Socio-Emotional Acts	Self Control	Averaged Ratings (Fifths)
1. Donald W.	5	3	1	1	3	2.6
2. Robert T.	2	4	4	1	2	2.6
3. Ray D.	5	4	1	1	4	3.0
4. Gene R.	1	5	3	5	5	3.8
5. George D.	5	4	2	1	2	2.8
6. John V.	3	2	3	1	1	2.0
7. Jim S.	2	4	4	1	4	3.0
8. Jerry M.	3	2	1	1	1	1.6
9. George A.	2	4	1	1	1	1.8
10. Robert B.	5	3	1	1	2	2.4
11. Joe F.	5	4	1	4	3	3.4
12. Pete S.	2	3	4	1	2	2.4
13. Ralph O.	3	1	1	1	2	1.6
14. William C.	5	5	1	1	2	2.8
15. Stan W.	1	2	2	1	4	2.0

Recasting the totals, the following clusters of averages emerge:

TOTAL		NAMES			
3.8		Gene R.	2.4		Robert B., Pete S.
3.6			2.2	C	
3.4	A	Joe F.	2.0		John V., Stan W.
3.2					
3.0		Ray D., Jim S.	1.8		George A.
			1.6	D	Jerry M., Ralph O.
2.8		George D., William C.			
2.6	B	Donald W., Robert T.			

VII.   Selecting Potential Members

In an attempt to create a balanced group of eight boys, we have arbitrarily divided the total into clusters of four (note broken lines) and decided to select two boys from each cluster. We first recalled (page 26) four factors that could lead to an ineffective group, (too much compatibility, too much stress, inadequate alternative models and negative sub-groups) and decided to try to avoid these difficulties in our selection. We also recalled (page 23) that an effective group consists of members who are interactive, compatible and mutually responsive.

Our selection process went something like this:

a. First we saw Gene as a potentially strong, positive group member. In wanting him "in" we decided to eliminate his two friends (danger of negative sub-group) John V. and Ralph O.

b. Since Gene R. had been known to initiate illegal acts, we decided to eliminate the other "high initiator," Stan W. to reduce potential stress.

c. William C. was chosen for his "skills and interests" since this could provide a good model for others.

d. Robert T. and Jim S. were selected because they had demonstrated task ability.

e. The fact that Gene and Jim S. were no longer on probation, and were apparently doing well, was an additional reason for wanting them in the group (as potential models for prosocial behavior).

The group then consisted of:

A. Gene R.
    Jim S.
_____

B. William C.
    Robert T.
_____

C. Robert B.
    Pete S.
_____

D. George A.
    Jerry M.
_____

In addition, Jerry M. was known to be uncomfortable around Blacks. Since this was to be a racially mixed group, it was decided to drop him from this group and lower the total to seven boys:

Gene R.
Jim S.
Donald W.
Robert T.
Robert B.
Pete S.
George A.

This was our "solution" to the problem. Perhaps yours is different—that is certainly possible. Obviously, no matter how "good" the composition is, the Group Worker must do his job effectively if the group is to achieve its objective.

The other boys might be formed into a second group, or they could be seen individually. They might also provide a pool for future members should any of these boys "graduate," fail (get in trouble again), or prove unworkable in this grouping.

You are to be congratulated for having come this far. Over the course of many revisions, we have become more and more aware of the broad range of issues affecting group composition. It's a complex business. Thanks for your interest and attention. We hope the program has been helpful, and would be interested in hearing about your experiences when you try to apply it to practice situations. Good luck!